OF BREATH
AND EARTH

OF BREATH AND EARTH

A BOOK OF DAYS
with wisdom from Native America

PHOTOGRAPHS AND COMPILATION BY
JOHN NETHERTON

Northland Publishing

Production supervised by Lisa Brownfield
Manufactured in Hong Kong by Wing King Tong

0489/5M/8-94

For my wife, Judy;
our children, Jason, Joshua, Erich, Joshua, and Evan;
and my parents, Mary and Hobert.

1

2

3

4

5

6

7

8

At the edge of the world

It is growing light.

Up rears the light.

Just yonder the day dawns,

Spreading over the night.

—TOHONO O'ODHAM SONG

10

11

12

13

14

15

16

17

18

19

20

21

What is life? It is the flash of a firefly in the night. It is the breath of a buffalo in the winter time. It is the little shadow which runs across the grass and loses itself in the sunset.

—CROWFOOT, BLACKFOOT

22

23

24

25

26

27

28

29

30

31

The ground on which we stand is sacred ground. It is the dust and blood of our ancestors.

—CHIEF PLENTY-COUPS, CROW

1

2

3

I know that our people possessed remarkable powers of concentration and abstraction, and I sometimes fancy that such nearness to nature as I have described keeps the spirit sensitive to impressions not commonly felt, and in touch with the unseen powers.

—OHIYESA (CHARLES ALEXANDER EASTMAN), SANTEE DAKOTA

4

5

6

7

8

9

10

11

Each soul must meet the morning sun, the new, sweet earth, and the Great Silence, alone!

—OHIYESA (CHARLES ALEXANDER EASTMAN), SANTEE DAKOTA

13

14

15

16

17

18

19

20

21

22

23

24

25

26

27

28

That our Earth Mother may wrap herself

In a fourfold robe of white meal,

That she may be covered with frost flowers,

That yonder on all the mossy mountains

The forests may huddle together with the cold,

That their arms may be broken by the snow,

In order that the land may be thus,

I have made my prayer sticks into living beings.

—ZUNI PRAYER OF OFFERING

1

2

3

4

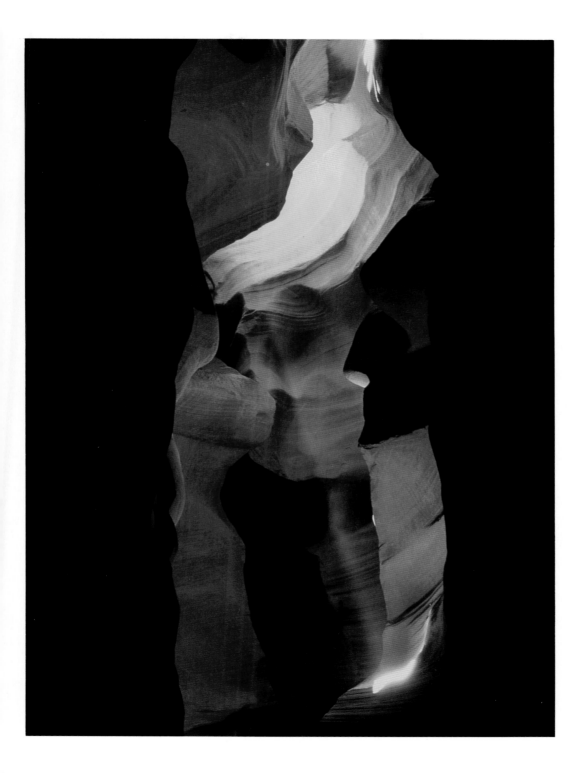

5

6

7

8

Kinship with all creatures of the earth, sky, and water was a real and active principle. For the animal and bird world there existed a brotherly feeling that kept the Lakota safe among them, and so close did some of the Lakotas come to their feathered and furred friends that in true brotherhood they spoke a common tongue.

—CHIEF LUTHER STANDING BEAR, LAKOTA

10

11

12

13

14

15

16

17

The Great Spirit is our father, but the earth is our mother. She nourishes us—that which we put into the ground she returns to us, and healing plants she gives us likewise. If we are wounded, we go to our mother and seek to lay the wounded part against her, to be healed. Animals, too, do thus—they lay their wounds to the earth.

—BEDAGI (BIG THUNDER), WABANAKIS NATION

18

19

20

21

22

23

24

25

26

27

28

29

30

31

Big Blue Mountain Spirit,

The home made of blue clouds,

The cross made of the blue mirage,

There, you have begun to live,

There, is the life of goodness,

I am grateful for that made of goodness there.

Big Yellow Mountain Spirit in the south,

Your spiritually hale body is made of yellow clouds;

Leader of the Mountain Spirits, holy Mountain Spirit,

You live by means of the good of this life

Big White Mountain Spirit in the west,

Your spiritually hale body is made of the white mirage;

Holy Mountain Spirit, leader of the Mountain Spirits,

I am happy over your words,

You are happy over my words.

Big Black Mountain Spirit in the north,

Your spiritually hale body is made of black clouds;

In that way, Big Black Mountain Spirit,

Holy Mountain Spirit, leader of the Mountain Spirits,

I am happy over your words,

You are happy over my words,

Now it is good.

—CHIRICAHUA PRAYER

1

2

3

4

5

6

7

8

9

10

11

12

13

14

15

16

17

18

By the sandy water I breathe in the odor of the sea; from there the wind comes and blows over the world.

—TOHONO O'ODHAM SONG

19

20

21

22

23

24

They listened to the warbling of birds and noted
the grandeur and the beauty of the forest. The
majestic clouds, which appear like mountains of
granite floating in the air; the golden tints of a
summer evening sky; and all the changes of nature
possessed a mysterious significance.

—BLACKBIRD (FRANCIS ASSIKINACK),
  OTTAWA

25

26

27

28

29

30

1

2

3

4

5

6

7

8

If the Great Spirit wanted men to stay in one place he would make the world stand still, but He made it to always change, so birds and animals can move and always have green grass and ripe berries; sunlight to work and play, and night to sleep; summer for flowers to bloom, and winter for them to sleep; always changing; everything for good; nothing for nothing.

—CHIEF FLYING HAWK, OGLALA SIOUX

9

10

11

12

13

14

15

16

Do you all help me!

My words are tied in one

With the great mountains,

With the great rocks,

With the great trees,

In one with my body

And my heart.

Do you all help me

With supernatural power

And you, day,

And you, night!

All of you see me

One with this world.

—YOKUTS PRAYER

17

18

19

20

21

22

23

24

25

26

27

28

Cover my earth mother four times with many flowers.

Let the heavens be covered with the banked-up clouds.

Let the earth be covered with fog; cover the earth with rains.

Great waters, rains, cover the earth. Lightning cover the earth.

Let thunder be heard over the earth; let thunder be heard;

Let thunder be heard over the six regions of the earth.

—ZUNI PRAYER

29

30

31

1

2

3

4

5

6

7

8

9

10

11

12

I was born upon the prairie where the wind blew free and there was nothing to break the light of the sun.
I was born where there were no enclosures and where everything drew a free breath. I want to die there,
not within walls.

—TEN BEARS, YAMPARIKA COMANCHE

13

14

15

16

17

18

19

20

21

22

23

24

25

26

27

28

29

The rainbow, a wreath over her brow, shall continue as long as the sun and the flowing of the river—while the work of art, however carefully protected and preserved, shall fade and crumble into dust.

—KAHGEGAGAHBOWH (GEORGE COPWAY), OJIBWA

1

2

3

4

5

6

7

8

On top of the mountain—

I do not myself know where—

I wandered where my mind

and my heart seemed to be lost.

I wandered away.

—TOHONO O'ODHAM
DREAM SONG

9

10

11

12

13

14

15

16

17

18

19

20

21

22

23

24

25

26

27

28

29

30

3 **1**

The man who sat on the ground in his tipi meditating on life and its meaning, accepting the kinship of all creatures, and acknowledging unity with the universe, was infusing into his being the true essence of civilization. And when native man left off this form of development, his humanization was retarded in growth.

—CHIEF LUTHER STANDING BEAR, LAKOTA

1

2

3

Butterfly, butterfly, butterfly, butterfly,

Oh, look, see it hovering among the flowers,

It is like a baby trying to walk and not knowing how to go.

The clouds sprinkle down the rain.

—ACOMA BUTTERFLY SONG

4

5

6

7

8

9

10

11

12

13

14

15

16

17

18

19

20

21

22

23

Everything as it moves, now and then, here and there, makes stops. The bird as it flies stops in one place to make its nest, and in another to rest in its flight. A man when he goes forth stops when he wills. So God has stopped. The sun, which is so bright and beautiful, is one place where He has stopped. The moon, the stars, the winds, He has been with. The trees, the animals, are all where He has stopped, and the Indian thinks of these places and sends his prayers there to reach the place where the god has stopped, and wins help and a blessing.

—DAKOTA WISEMAN

24

25

26

27

28

29

30

31

1

2

3

4

5

6

7

8

9

10

11

12

From my boyhood I have observed leaves, trees, and grass, and I have never found two alike. They may have a general likeness, but on examination I have found that they differ slightly. Plants are of different families.... It is the same with animals.... It is the same with human beings. There is some place which is best adapted to each. The seeds of the plants are blown about by the wind until they reach the place where they will grow best—where the action of the sun and the presence of moisture are most favorable to them, and there they take root and grow.

—OKUTE (SHOOTER), TETON SIOUX

13

14

15

16

17

18

19

20

All living creatures and all plants are a benefit to something. Certain animals fulfill their purpose by definite acts. The crows, buzzards, and flies are somewhat similar in their use, and even the snakes have purpose in being. In the early days the animals probably roamed over a very wide country until they found a proper place. An animal depends a great deal on the natural conditions around it. If the buffalo were here today, I think they would be different from the buffalo of the old days because all the natural conditions have changed. They would not find the same food, nor the same surroundings. We see the changes in our ponies—in the old days they could stand great hardship and travel long distance without water; they lived on certain kinds of food and drank pure water. Now our horses require a mixture of food; they have less endurance and must have constant care.

—OKUTE (SHOOTER), TETON SIOUX

21

22

23

24

25

26

27

28

It was the wind that gave them life. It is the wind that comes out of our mouths now that gives us life. When this ceases to blow, we die. In the skin at the tips of our fingers we see the trail of the wind; it shows us where the wind blew when our ancestors were created.

—NAVAJO LEGEND

29

30

1

2

3

4

5

6

7

8

9

10

11

12

I was born in Nature's wide domain! The trees were all that sheltered my infant limbs, the blue heavens all

that covered me. I am one of Nature's children. I have always admired her. She shall be my glory: her features,

her robes, and the wreath about her brow; the seasons, her stately oaks, and the evergreen; her hair, ringlets

over the earth, all contribute to my enduring love of her.

—CHIEF PLENTY-COUPS, CROW

14

15

16

17

18

19

20

21

22

23

24

25

26

27

28

29

30

31

1

2

3

4

5

6

7

8

Over there, far off, he runs

With his white forefeet

Through the brush.

Over there, nearby, he runs,

With his nostrils open,

Over the bare ground.

The white tail, climbing,

Seems like a streak on the rocks.

The black tail, striding,

Seems like a crack in the rocks.

—TOHONO O'ODHAM SONG

9

10

11

12

13

14

15

16

17

18

A man ought to desire that which is genuine instead of that which is artificial. Long ago there was no such thing as a mixture of earths to make paint. There were only three colors of native earth paint—red, white, and black. These could be obtained only in certain places. When other colors were desired, the Indians mixed the juices of plants, but it was found that these mixed colors faded and it could always be told when the red was genuine—the red made of burned clay.

—OKUTE (SHOOTER), TETON SIOUX

19

20

21

22

23

24

25

26

27

28

29

30

She continues her spiritual teaching ... in whispered songs, bird-like, at morning and evening. To her and to the child the birds are real people, who live very close to the Great Mystery; the murmuring trees breathe its presence; the falling waters chant its praise.

—OHIYESA (CHARLES ALEXANDER EASTMAN), SANTEE DAKOTA

1

2

3

4

5

6

7

8

9

10

11

12

Along the entire length and breadth

of the earth, our grandmother

extended the green reflection

of her covering,

and the escaping odors

were pleasant to inhale.

—WINNEBAGO POEM

14

15

16

17

18

19

20

21

22

23

24

25

26

27

28

29

White floating clouds,

Clouds like the plains,

Come and water the earth.

—ZIA RAIN SONG

30

31

BIBLIOGRAPHY

Bunzel, Ruth. *Introduction to Zuñi Ceremonialism*. Bureau of American
      Ethnology 47th Annual Report, 1929—30.

Curtis, Natalie. *The Indian's Book*. Harper and Brother, 1907.

Densmore, Frances. *Music of Acoma, Isleta, Cochiti, and Zuñi Pueblos*.
      Bureau of American Ethnology Bulletin 165, 1957.

———. *Papago Music*. Bureau of American Ethnology Bulletin 90, 1929.

Dixon, Joseph K. *The Vanishing Race*. Doubleday, 1913.

Dorsey, James Owen. *A Study of Siouan Cults*. Bureau of American
      Ethnology 11th Annual Report, 1889—1890.

Eastman, Charles Alexander (Ohiyesa). *The Soul of the Indian*. Houghton
      Mifflin, 1911.

Hoijer, Harry. *Chiricahua and Mescalero Apache Texts*. University of
      Chicago Press, 1938.

Jacobs, Paul, and Saul Landau, with Eve Pell. *To Serve the Devil*, vol. 1.
      Vintage Books, 1971.

Kroeber, Al. *Handbook of the Indians of California*. Bureau of American
      Ethnology Bulletin 78, 1925.

MacEwan, Grant. *Tatanga Mani: Walking Buffalo of the Stonies*.
      MJ Hurtig, Ltd., 1969.

Matthews, Washington. *Navaho Legends*. 1897.

McCreight, M. I. *Firewater and Forked Tongues*. Trail's End Publishing
      Company, 1947.

Monture, Ethel Brant. *Canadian Portraits: Brant, Crowfoot, Oronhyatekha,
      Famous Indians*. Clarke, Irwin, and Company, 1960.

Radin, Paul. *The Road of Life and Death*. Princeton University Press, 1945.

Standing Bear, Chief Luther. *Land of the Spotted Eagle*. Houghton
      Mifflin, 1933.

Stevenson, M. C. *The Zuñi Indians*. Bureau of American Ethnology 23rd
      Annual Report, 1901—02.

Underhill, Ruth. *Singing for Power*. University of California Press, 1938.

Just as the quotes JOHN NETHERTON compiled for *Of Breath and Earth* are a record of the Native American philosophy of living in harmony with the land, John's photography reflects a personal philosophy of respect for nature. He has been recording the natural world with passion and sensitivity for more than 25 years.

John lives in his native Tennessee with his wife; together they have five sons. He has studied with such greats as Ansel Adams, Eliot Porter, and Ernst Haas. He is a columnist for *Outdoor Photographer*, and his work has been published in such periodicals as *Audubon, Natural History, National Wildlife, International Wildlife, National Geographic*, and numerous others. His books include *Radnor Lake: Nashville's Walden; Tennessee: A Homecoming; A Guide to Photography and the Smoky Mountains; Florida: A Guide to Nature and Photography; Big South Fork Country; Tennessee Wonders*; and *At the Water's Edge*.

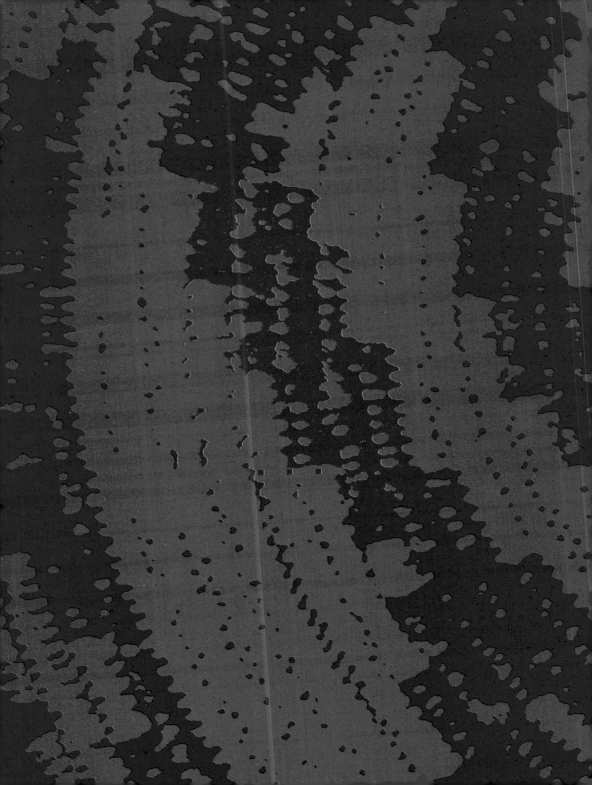